What Happens When I Yawn?

By Aleaha Schwinn

Gareth Stevens
Publishing

Please visit our website, www.garethstevens.com. For a free color catalog of all our high-quality books, call toll free 1-800-542-2595 or fax 1-877-542-2596.

Library of Congress Cataloging-in-Publication Data

Schwinn, Aleaha.
What happens when I yawn? / by Aleaha Schwinn.
p. cm. — (My body does strange stuff)
Includes index.
ISBN 978-1-4339-9358-9 (pbk.)
ISBN 978-1-4339-9359-6 (6-pack)
ISBN 978-1-4339-9357-2 (library binding)
1. Reflexes—Juvenile literature. 2. Respiration—Juvenile literature. I. Title.
QP372. S39 2014
612.8—dc23

Published in 2014 by
Gareth Stevens Publishing
111 East 14th Street, Suite 349
New York, NY 10003

Designer: Michael J. Flynn
Editor: Greg Roza

Photo credits: Cover Kameel4u/Shutterstock.com; p. 5 Jupiterimages/Thinkstock.com; p. 7 CLIPAREA/Shutterstock.com; p. 9 Dorling Kindersley/Getty Images; p. 11 Rob Lewine/Getty Images; p. 13 DuleS/Shutterstock.com; p. 15 Monkee Business/Thinkstock.com; p. 17 Geoffrey Kuchera/Shutterstock.com; p. 19 Thinkstock.com; p. 21 OJO Images/Getty Images.

Printed in the United States of America

CPSIA compliance information: Batch #CS13GS: For further information contact Gareth Stevens, New York, New York at 1-800-542-2595.

Contents

Boldface words appear in the glossary.

Close Your Mouth!

You might yawn when you stay up late or just after getting out of bed. Many people yawn when they're bored. Or you might yawn because someone else just did! **Scientists** aren't exactly sure why we yawn. However, they have a few interesting ideas.

How It Works

A small part on the bottom of the brain controls many of the body's activities, including yawning. This part of the brain sends messages out to the body and makes it yawn.

brain

7

When we yawn, our brain tells **muscles** all over the body to work. The mouth opens wide to let in a lot of air. Muscles around the lungs help us take a deep breath. After a short pause, these muscles push the air back out of the lungs.

I Didn't Mean to Do It!

Yawning is involuntary. That means our bodies do it without us choosing to do so. We know it's involuntary because babies do it before they're born. You may even find yourself yawning just because you saw a picture of someone yawning!

Why Do We Do It?

When we breathe in, we take in oxygen, which our body needs to keep working. When we breathe out, our body gets rid of a waste gas called carbon dioxide. We might yawn to get more oxygen into our bodies or to get rid of extra carbon dioxide.

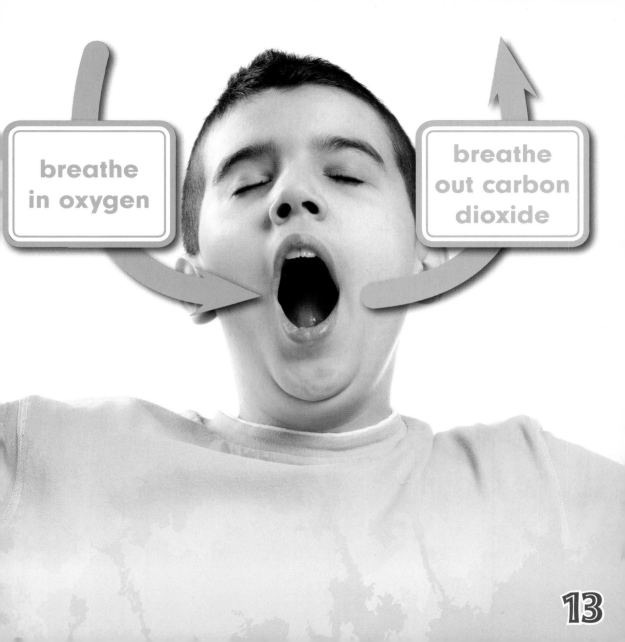

13

Many scientists think we yawn to cool off our brain. Yawning increases blood flow in the head. The air we breathe in during a yawn cools the blood that passes close to the mouth. This cooler blood may then help cool the brain.

Many animals yawn, but only people, chimps, and dogs yawn when they see others do it. Some scientists now think this shows you care about others around you. Yawning might be a way of sharing our feelings.

17

Some scientists think yawning might be something people long, long ago did to **communicate** and the habit just stuck with us. Perhaps people once yawned to show their teeth and scare enemies away, somewhat like many wild animals do.

take in oxygen, get rid of carbon dioxide

cool off the brain

WHY DO YOU THINK PEOPLE YAWN?

share feelings with others

old way of communicating

19

Yawning Too Much?

In **rare** cases, someone who yawns all the time might have a problem worse than being tired or bored. For example, it could be a sign of heart problems. If you can't stop yawning, it's a good idea to go see a doctor.

Glossary

communicate: to share thoughts or feelings by sound, movement, or writing

muscle: one of the parts of the body that allow movement

rare: uncommon or special

scientist: someone who studies the way things work and the way things are

For More Information

Books

Conrad, David. *Burps, Boogers, and Other Body Functions.* Mankato, MN: Capstone Press, 2012.

Nicolson, Cynthia Pratt. *Totally Human: Why We Look and Act the Way We Do.* Tonawanda, NY: Kids Can Press, 2011.

Stangl, Jean. *What Makes You Cough, Sneeze, Burp, Hiccup, Blink, Yawn, Sweat, and Shiver?* New York, NY: Franklin Watts, 2000.

Websites

KidsHealth
kidshealth.org/kid
Find more information about yawning and many other health topics.

Yawning
www.cyh.com/HealthTopics/HealthTopicDetailsKids. aspx?p=335&np=152&id=2454
Learn more about yawning, including some other interesting theories.

Publisher's note to educators and parents: Our editors have carefully reviewed these websites to ensure that they are suitable for students. Many websites change frequently, however, and we cannot guarantee that a site's future contents will continue to meet our high standards of quality and educational value. Be advised that students should be closely supervised whenever they access the Internet.

Index